D1410578

Hi, welcome to the fun way to learn about Halloween through 100 creative coloring pages!

Ideally suited for kids ages 1-4 as they discover the world around them. This book is intended to boost early childhood development through engaging activities that build connections with words, pictures and colors. All the custom artwork has been created by experienced designers to be the right level for kids to stimulate imagination, to allow them to build their fine motor skills and to have a load of fun and learning in the process!

With 100 big pages of illustrations, children will explore and enjoy a HUGE variety of easy to color Halloween designs.

Thank you for purchasing this book and we hope you and your little ones unlock a world of coloring fun and learning!
We're still learning and growing ourselves, so we'd really appreciate a review on Amazon for this book if you have time.
Thank you

Check out other titles in our TODDLER COLORING series!

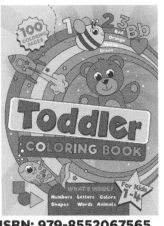

ISBN: 979-8552067565   ISBN: 979-8509492808

We hope you enjoyed this book. As we learn and grow, we'd love a rating or review for it on Amazon, if you have time. *Thank You!*

Loads more from Under The Cover Press
available at **amazon**

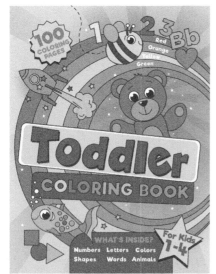

ISBN 979-8552067565

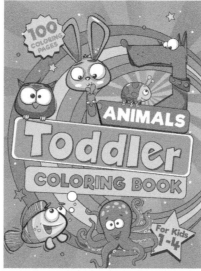

ISBN 979-8509492808

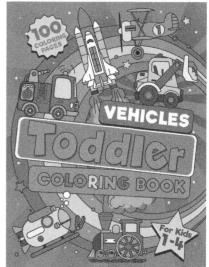

ISBN 979-8520557715

ISBN 979-8590346219

ISBN 979-8695161878

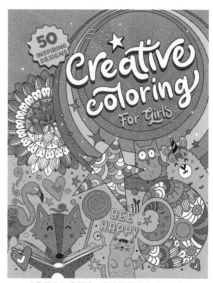

ISBN 979-8575406419

ISBN 979-8559845876

ISBN 979-8559850436

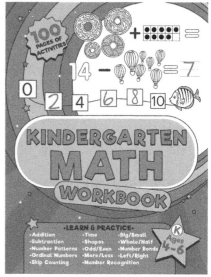

ISBN 979-8717778565

READY FOR
TRICK OR TREAT

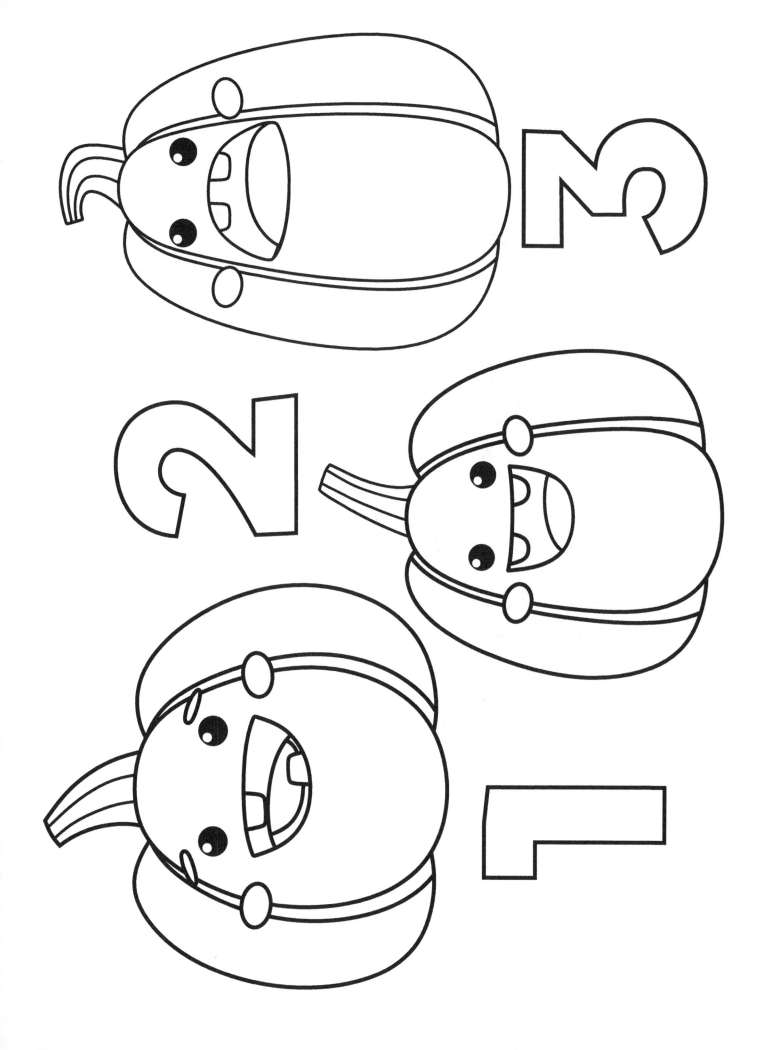

Happy Halloween

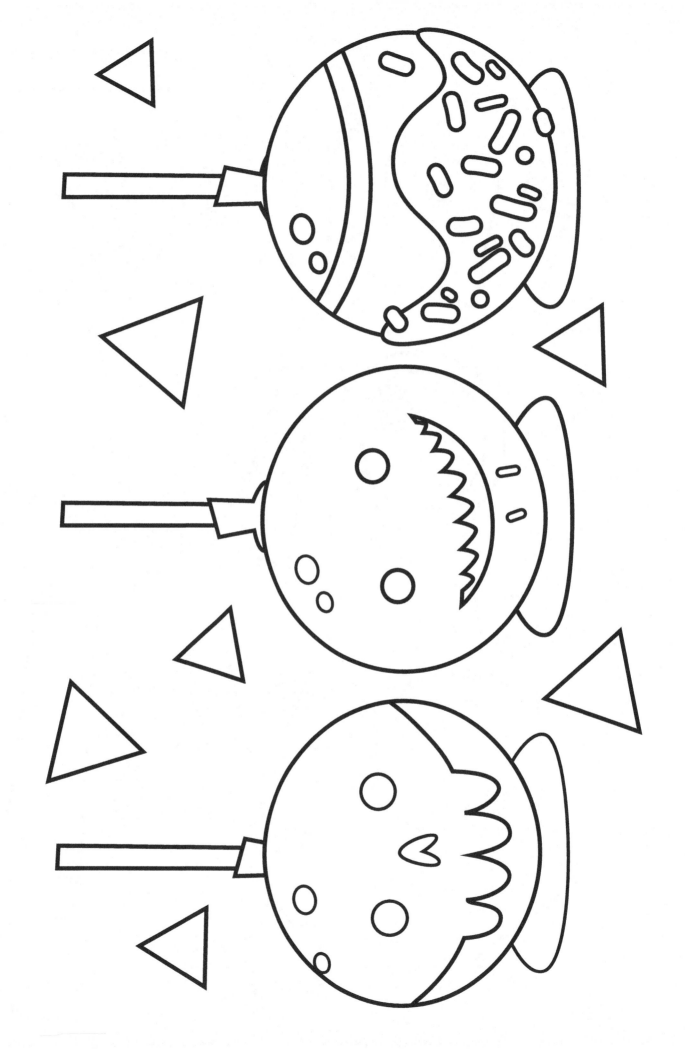

PUMPKIN

MONSTER

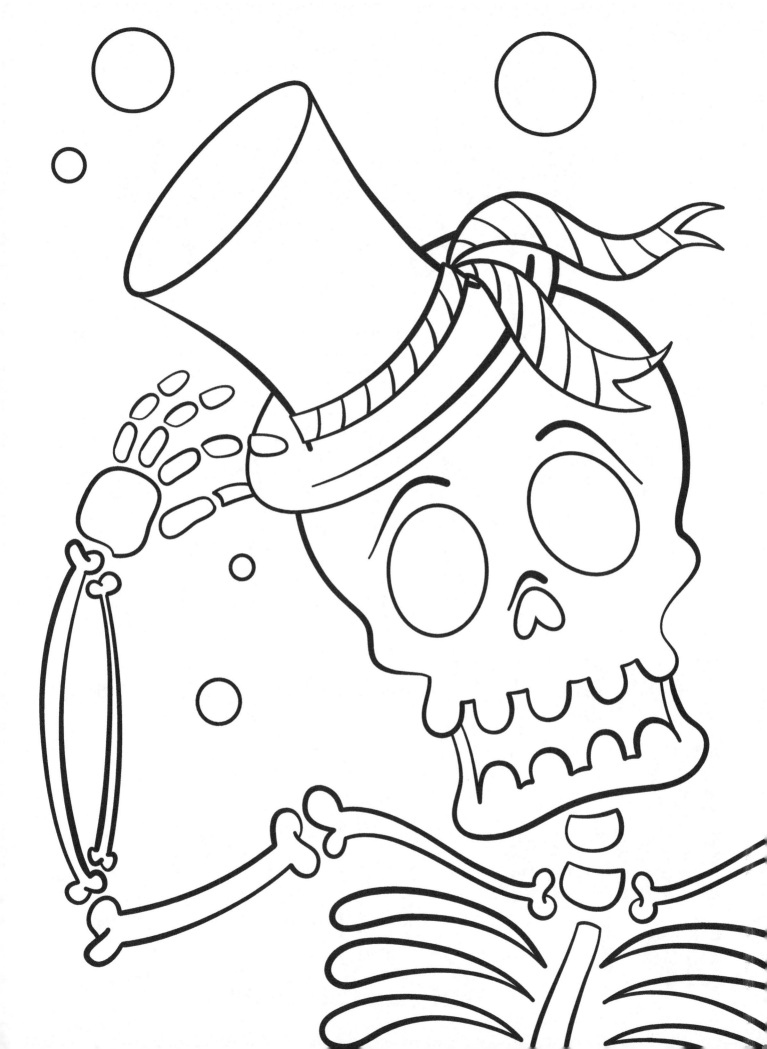

TIME
TO
DRESS
UP !

WHAT'S YOUR SILLY MONSTER FACE?

HALLOWEEN DANCE PARTY!

TIME
TO
DRESS
UP !

CAULDRON

TIME
TO
DRESS
UP !

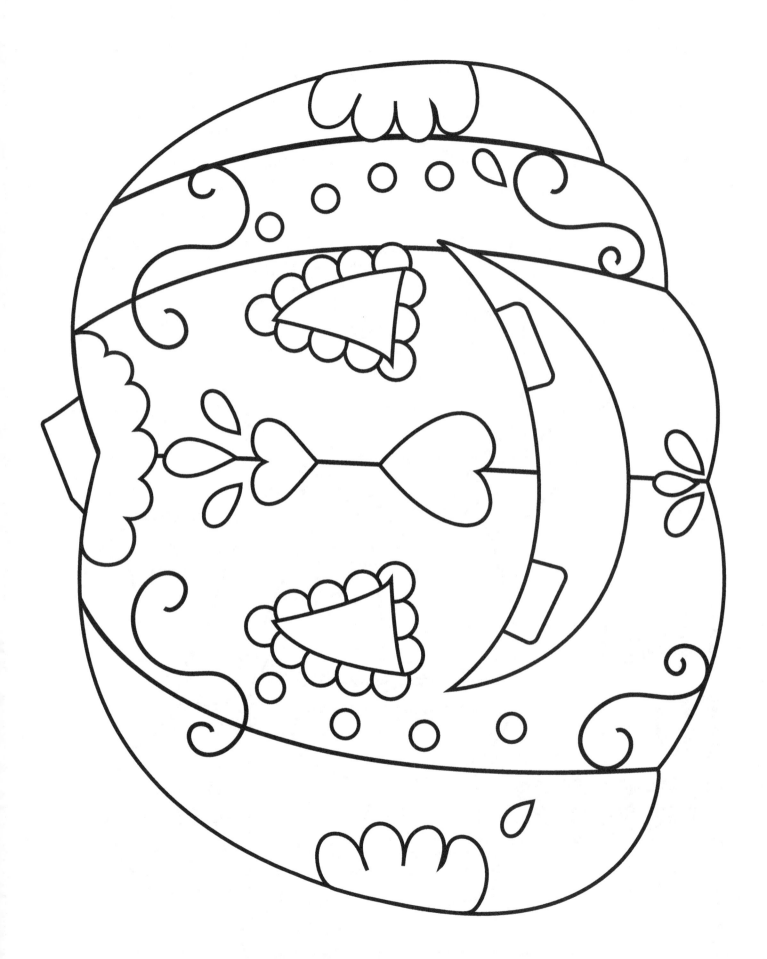

TRICK OR TREAT

SPOOKY
SCARECROW

TIME TO DRESS UP !

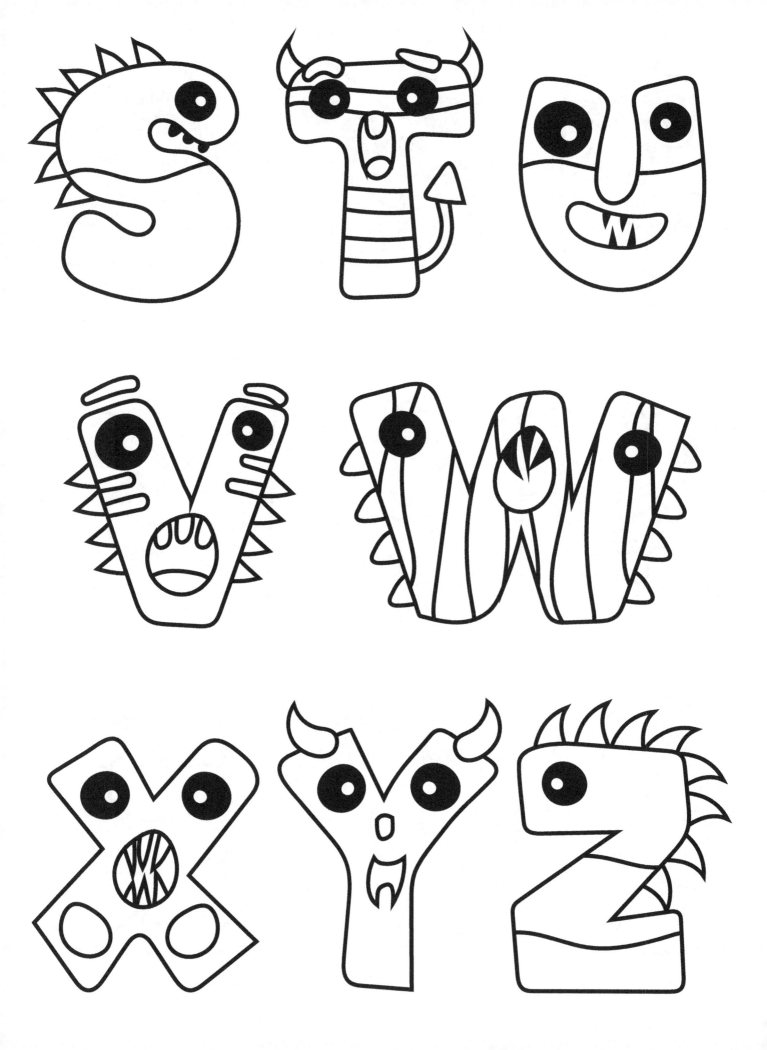

DRAW & COLOR YOUR OWN PUMPKIN DESIGN ON BOTH SIDES OF THE PAPER. ASK A GROWN-UP TO CAREFULLY CUT IT OUT AND DISPLAY!

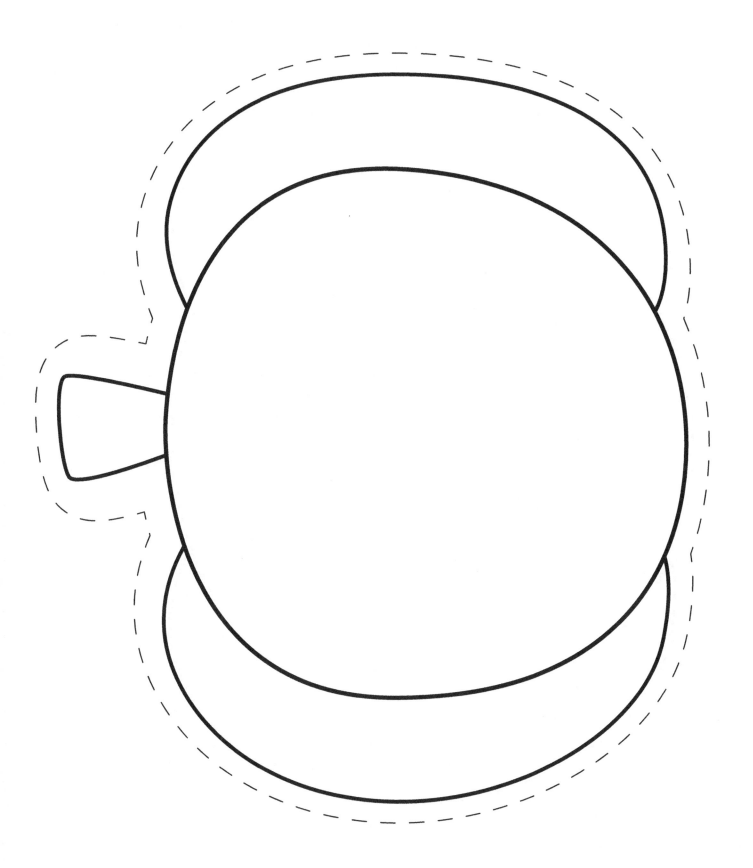

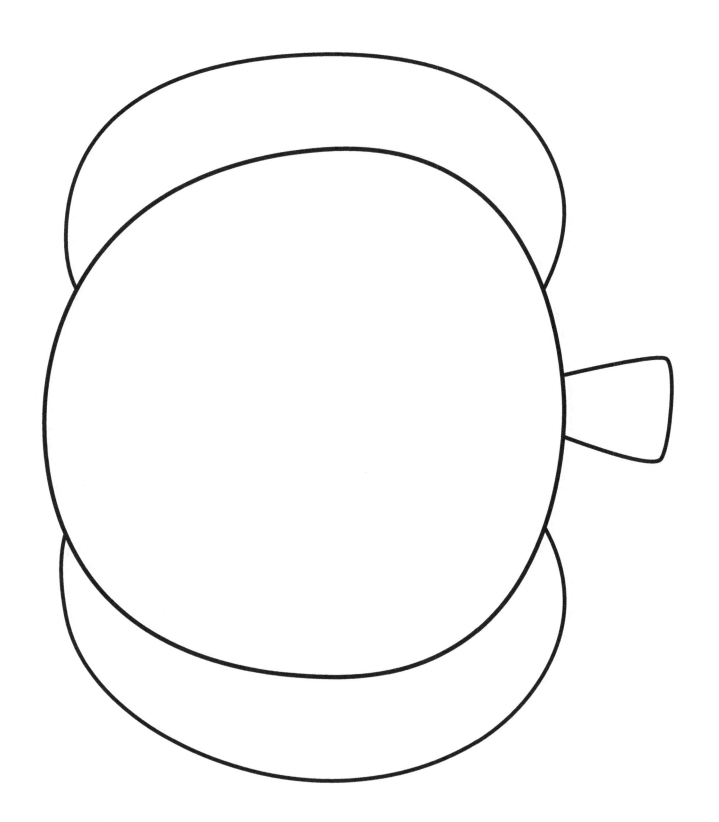

This HALLOWEEN Toddler COLORING BOOK

BELONGS TO

 **100** pages full of age-appropriate, easy to color designs.

PUMPKINS • TREATS • SILLY MONSTERS • CATS
• OWLS • BATS • COSTUMES •

Coloring and learning has never been so much fun!

Includes these pages and many, many more...

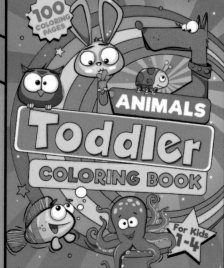

CHECK OUT OTHER TITLES IN OUR
TODDLER COLORING
SERIES!

EVEN MORE **100** PAGE,
BIG COLORING BOOKS.

GROWN UPS!
VISIT US AT
UnderTheCoverPress.com
OR SCAN TO VISIT US

FREE STUFF • NEWS • INI

ISBN: 979-8552067565   ISBN: 979-8509492808

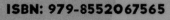

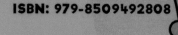
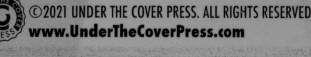
ISBN 9798548451484

9798548451484
9 00